Churchill

Polar bears were once thought to be solitary animals that would avoid contact with other bears except for mating. In the Churchill region, however, many alliances between bears are made in the fall. These friendships last only until the ice forms, then its every bear for himself as they hunt the seals.

CHURCHILL

Polar Bear Capital of the World

by Mark Fleming

HYPERION PRESS LIMITED
1988

Cover photograph courtesy of Mike Macri

Photographs on pages 4 and 5
courtesy of Dave LeGros

Hyperion Press Limited gratefully acknowledges
the continued support of the Manitoba Arts
Council and Canada Council.

ISBN: 0-920534-74-0

Design by A. O. Osen
Typography by Raeber Graphics Inc.
Color separations by G.B. Graphics Inc.
Printing by Premier Printing Ltd.

PRINTED IN CANADA

Dedication

This book is dedicated in part to those intrepid adventurers, the tourists, who yearly make the trek to Churchill. Since their visits are necessarily short, I thought it would be fitting if they could take away with them some idea of what life is like here year round, as well as a reminder of the new and exciting things they witnessed while they were here.

More importantly, this book is a tribute to the people of Churchill — the trappers and tugboat captains, shop clerks and waitresses, grain handlers and railroad workers, bank tellers and store owners, truck drivers and inn keepers, police and teachers, doctors and nurses, artists and carpenters — all the men, women, and children, newcomers and oldtimers, Indian, Métis, Inuit, black, and white. They are a rare and eclectic blend of people, typified only by their strength and pride, humor and determination, vision and imagination. For while Churchill is distinguished by the rugged beauty of its surroundings, it is its people that make it a truly special place to be.

Contents

Acknowledgments

I would like to thank the many people who have assisted in making this book a reality. A special thanks goes to Dave LeGros, who contributed numerous photographs and shared the trials and tribulations of publishing my first book. And thanks to our fellow photographers — Lorraine Skibo, Brian Turner, Howard Wilson, Mike Macri, Diane Erickson, Lorraine Brandson, Paul Watts, Manitoba Department of Natural Resources officers Don Jacobs and Ian Thorleifson. I am also grateful for contributions from the Manitoba Archives and Canadian National Railway.

More than 500 hours of research went into this publication and dozens of people in Churchill contributed stories and information — most notably Mike Macri, Penny Rawlings, Ed and Hanna Bazlik, Lily MacAuley, Howard Wilson, Lorne Robb, Bonnie Chartier, Brian Ladoon, Dr. Patrick Brown, Roy Bukowsky, Sigrun Martin, and Al Wokes. And many thanks again to Lorraine Brandson for her unselfish efforts in uncovering many of the facts contained in these pages.

Special thanks are also due to my friends and especially my family who have supported me throughout the making of this book and who believed that it would all come out all right in the end even when I had some doubts. I must thank my grandmothers who taught me to work hard and never give up, my parents who have supported me in all my endeavors, and my wife Kim and children Mandy and Markie who were always there as an often-needed distraction and as willing subjects in many photographs. Thank you. I love you all.

Lastly, this book would not have been possible without the special assistance of
Jack and Audrey O'Connor
The Manitoba Metis Federation
The Tundra Inn: Robert and Pat Penwarden
William Calnan
Elizabeth Brenner
Edgar's Place: Edgar Botelho
Les Tutkaluke and Pam Choptain
Seaport Hotel: Tony and Maria Correia
Dr. Norbert Froese
Churchill Health Centre Entertainment Committee
Rose Kennedy
Carol Mathews and Brian Ladoon
Herbert Spence
Michael and Sharon Woods
Susan Courtney and Steacy Courtney
Susan Derk
Wendy, Ian, and Tracy MacDonald
Reverend and Mrs. Caskey
Arctic Trading Company: Penny Rawlings
Brian McTaggart
Jim and Nancy Clark
Barbara and Maciej Ksiazkiewicz
Vicky and Glen McEwan
Gerry and Mandalena Clyke
Monique, Randy, and Christopher Neuls
Churchill Wilderness Encounters
Dr. Mike Figurski
Andrea Iwanowsky
Toni and Mark Therens
from Churchill, Manitoba,

Terry and Janet Williams
Jim and Cathy Douglas
Kay Wolanik
Brian Turner
Helen Beeston
Dodi Sherratt
Dianne, Neal, and Amber Fisher
from Winnipeg, Manitoba,

Joe and Carole Fleming
Grant Fleming
Kevin Fleming
Nurco Holdings: Bill and Carol Nurcombe
from Calgary, Alberta,

Leslie and Maurice DeMargerie
from Lorette, Manitoba,

Haley Shannon Watson
from Toronto, Ontario,

Wendy Sherrat and Oscar Suarez Family
from Denver, Colorado,

Mildred Kelly
from Winnipeg Beach, Manitoba,

Bill and Joan Sherratt
from Lintlaw, Saskatchewan.

Not so long ago, if you mentioned that you lived in Churchill, Manitoba, you'd get a blank stare by way of reply. Mention Churchill now, however, and you'll probably be greeted with a smile of recognition. "Of course. That's where the polar bears live."

Well, no, it's not — although it's true that the annual convergence of hundreds of bears on a point of land just outside the town (and their occasional forays into it) has earned Churchill the nickname "Polar Bear Capital of the World."

But Churchill is known by many names. To prairie farmers, railway workers, and merchant seamen it's Canada's northernmost seaport and grain-handling centre. To ornithologists and marine biologists it's a birder's and whale watcher's paradise. And to the thousand people whose work and lives are centred here, it's home.

The area where Churchill is situated, some 1126 kilometres (700 miles) north of Manitoba's capital, Winnipeg, has seen human habitations come and go for at least 4000 years by archeological reckonings. Long before the 1700s when Europeans made their first landings in the area on quests for the elusive Northwest Passage to the Orient, native Inuit and Indian tribes often made camp where the Churchill River flows into Hudson Bay.

In the past 400 years the area around Churchill has been the site of a Hudson's Bay trading post, a British fort, an astronomical observatory, a rocket range, a modern military installation, and the thriving township that survives to this day.

It's this modern town that is the focus of this book. In many ways it's just like any small community. People here go through the day-to-day routines common to people all over the world.

They do it in weather that can range from a summertime high of 33.9°C (93.0°F) to a bone chilling low of -45.6°C (-50.1°F) — and that's not counting the record windchill of 2950 watts/meter (yard) squared. (Exposed skin can freeze in less than a minute when the windchill hits 1600.)

And they do it in a land so remote from other bastions of civilization that they routinely joke about trading their first born for fresh produce or losing them to mosquitoes and black flies so large that the Department of Transport requires them to have identification numbers under their wings.

These people are, without a doubt, an odd admixture of human beings. Natives whose ancestors hunted and fished here for countless generations play bingo beside brand new immigrants from countries that might as well be light years away. Kids who are accustomed to hanging out at big city shopping malls learn how to have fun all over again from kids who have never seen the inside of a fast food restaurant.

Churchill is a place tempered by extremes and characterized by contrasts. It's a town less than 60-years old in an area as rich in historic detail as any-where in Canada. It boasts a multi-million dollar, fully modern health and recreation complex that any urban industrial centre would envy, set amidst some of this planet's most uncompromisingly rugged wilderness. Life here depends on both the latest in technology and the most traditional of skills.

If none of this is readily apparent to the casual eye of the visitor, it's not surprising. He's probably looking nervously over his shoulder to see if there's a bear behind him.

It's not till you've passed a few seasons here and become accustomed to (though never blasé about) the astonishing array of surprises Mother Nature dishes up on a daily basis, that you begin to understand the essential duality of Churchill. You get your first hint on arrival when you realize that the strength and toughness of the people here is only equalled by their warmth and their willingness to help the tenderfoot newcomer. And it truly comes home to you when you are about to leave Churchill. You think of all the things you've cursed every year — the snow you shovelled endlessly, the bugs that considered you a never-ending smorgasborg, the unavailability of things taken for granted everywhere else, and the outrageous prices of the things that you could get — and you begin to think how much you'll miss them all.

Suddenly the trapper heading out to check his trapline on his late-model all-terrain vehicle or skinning his catch as an F-4 Phantom Jet creates sonic booms overhead makes perfect sense. In Churchill the most widely opposing forces can come together in unique harmony.

For all those people who only get to see one facet of Churchill during their all too short vacation, this book offers a glimpse of the town during the rest of the year.

And for those who live here now, it's an affectionate thank you from this newcomer who hopes he has become as much a part of Churchill as it has become a part of him.

Why would anyone build a town way up there?

Situated on a narrow strip of land surrounded by water, north of the timberline, and a full one thousand and twelve rail miles from major population centres, Churchill's location appears to have been picked by some quixotic hermit with a passion for hardship.

It really has to do with grain. The prairie provinces are the breadbasket of the world, but their efficiency in delivering the goods to the world market was hampered by having to ship everything halfway across the country to the Great Lakes in Ontario. A prairie seaport was needed and Manitoba's northern coastline was the only place to build one.

The Hudson Bay Railway line to Churchill was integrated into the Canadian National Railway in 1930. Although the line originally was heading farther south toward York Factory at the mouth of the Nelson River it veered north when it was discovered that the harbor there couldn't handle ocean-going vessels. It made its way toward the more accommodating harbor afforded by the Churchill River — and the town of Churchill was born.

It took 3000 men working at a frantic pace to complete the 70,000 metric tonnes (2.5 million-bushel) capacity grain handling facility by 1931. (A further 70,000 metric tonnes or 2.5 million-bushel storage facility was added in 1955.) The elevator and loading docks had to be constructed and the harbor dredged, and thousands of tons of equipment had to be transported — much of it brought from the mouth of the Nelson River over roads built on the bay ice before the railway arrived.

Howard Wilson was one of the workers during 1931. He labored 9 to 10 hours per day for 42.5 cents per hour or about $100 per month after living expenses were deducted.

"And I was damn glad to get that," says Wilson now 78. "Those were darn good wages for a young man in the depression years."

Wilson reports that while there was lots of work in Churchill, living was hard there in other ways. To discourage gambling the Department of Railways and Canals gave the men only $5 cash each month, depositing the rest of their wages in their banks at home. Some gambled away their cash anyway and went penniless the rest of the month. There was also no liquor and no women allowed in town. The only way out was to quit and hop the supply train headed south. (Fine, old-fashioned entrepreneurial spirit held sway, however, as a trading post was established on the west side of the river. Later another business appeared, a "house of pleasure.")

A token one-ton load of wheat was shipped from the Port of Churchill in 1929. It was a sort of public relations move, but Wilson was there when the first real commercial shipment (277 thousand bushels) left Churchill aboard the *SS Farnsworth* out of England. That's a far cry from the 43,500 metric tonnes (1.6 million bushels) carried by the freight liner *Berhard Oldendorff*, the

Over 2,000 men were employed with the construction of the grain elevator and dock and there were always jobs available, even in the Depression.

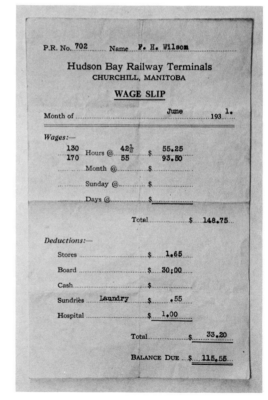

P.R. No. 702   Name F. H. Wilson

Hudson Bay Railway Terminals
CHURCHILL, MANITOBA

WAGE SLIP

Month of .... June .... 193 1.

Wages:—

130	Hours @	42½	$ 55.25
170		55	$ 93.50
	Month @		$
	Sunday @		$
	Days @		$

Total .... $ 148.75

Deductions:—

Stores		$ 1.65
Board		$ 30.00
Cash		$
Sundries	Laundry	$ .55
Hospital		$ 1.00

Total .... $ 33.20

BALANCE DUE ... $ 115.55

H. Wilson

The building of the port signaled a new era for Churchill.

H. Wilson

Howard Wilson stands beside a grain freighter being loaded at the dock he helped to build.

Churchill train station constructed in 1943.

Manitoba Archives

14 largest ship ever to dock in Churchill. As many as 58 ships have jockeyed for position at the port during the short shipping season.

That season is, of course, during the fall months when dock workers, grain handlers, and ships crews race to get the barley and wheat harvests loaded and shipped before freeze-up by the end of October. Some ships with ice-breaking capability have left port later in the year. One Canadian ship, *MV Arctic*, didn't depart until November 17 in 1979.

The first time Europeans hove in sight of what would ultimately become Churchill was 1612, when the British explorer Captain Thomas Button sailed into Hudson Bay hoping to find the Northwest Passage. He didn't. He also missed out on discovering the mouth of the Churchill River which he sailed past twice without noticing.

That honor would fall to Danish adventurer Jens Munck, who might be forgiven if he didn't think it was worth it all. He landed his 2 ships at the mouth of the river in 1619 and spent the winter there, losing all but two of his crew to scurvy, trichinosis, and exposure. He had to abandon one of his ships and, with the two survivors, sail the smaller craft, the *Lamprey*, back to Denmark — a feat nothing short of miraculous.

Of course, Henry Hudson had pre-ceded these stalwarts into the area in 1610, having the Bay named after him in the process, but also suffering a full-scale mutiny which left him cast adrift near Charlton Island in James Bay.

A mountain of liquid gold pours into the hold of a freighter. As this ship is loaded other ships wait in the bay for permission to dock. Usually only 2 ships are allowed in port at one time (p. 14).

By fall Churchill's international sea port is bustling with activity as ships dock to load with grain. Ships must leave before the end of October freeze-up unless they have ice-breaking capabilities.

The tugboat George Kidd is dwarfed by the Nymph C, a freighter of Greek origin.

This ship won't run aground! The deep river channel averages 16 metres (50 ft) but the low tidal flats in the foreground make the river depth deceptive (p. 16).

Churchill's short shipping season from late July to late October means long days and someone always gets the sunset docking time. This Russian freighter docks with the assistance of the George Kidd and the W. N. Twolan (p. 17).

D. LeGros

18   It wasn't until 1717 that the Hudson's Bay Company established a trading post on the west shore of the Churchill River and, in 1732, began constructing Fort Prince of Wales, a task that would consume 40 years. This massive structure had walls 12 metres (40 feet) thick and 5 metres (16 feet) high with 40 mounted guns, all designed to keep the rival French fur traders out of the lucrative Hudson Bay area.

Ironically, this fort, one of the most massive stone structures on the continent, fell to the French in 1783 without a single shot being fired. Governor Samuel Hearne and his 40-man garrison were outnumbered and had to surrender. The French burned all the interior buildings and tried to disable the fort by exploding charges in the mouths of the cannons and blowing up the outer walls. The fort was returned to the British but no attempt was made to reoccupy it and it lay in ruins until the Canadian government began restoring it in the 1930s.

Samuel Hearne's name, which he painstakingly etched in flowing script on a rock at Sloop's Cove, 2 kilometres upriver from Fort Prince of Wales, is well known to any Canadian schoolchild. The extraordinary explorer made an overland trek to where the Coppermine River flows into the Arctic Ocean, reaching it, after three tries, in 1771. He served as governor of the fort from 1775 to 1787 and died five years later at the age of 47.

It's hard to believe that the pile of rubble by the side of the airport road

D. LeGros

D. LeGros

Masonry and concrete were used to restore the Fort to its original condition (p. 18).

Samuel Hearne was governor of the Fort from 1775 to 1787. On an early visit to Sloop's Cove he etched his name in the rock.

In the 18th C the Fort was mounted with 40 cannon but they were never fired in battle.

Ruins of Fort Prince of Wales in 1933 after 150 years of neglect.

D. LeGros

Manitoba Archives

has been cleaned up now and all that's left of Fort Churchill is a few buildings and a flat open space. At one time it was the largest joint Canada-U.S. military installation in the world. Built in 1942 as a response to the threat posed by German submarines rumored to have been spotted in the Hudson Strait at various times during WW II, it grew into a miniature metropolis complete with its own 620-seat movie theatre, bakery, post office, gift shop, bowling alley, hockey rink, and hospital — plus chapels and schools. Heated walkways linked most of the buildings which were wired to two power supplies to insure there was never a blackout.

The town of Churchill, little more than a frontier trading post with no running water, sewage system, or street lights, counted no more than 150 souls after the construction crews finished their work and left. It experienced a major boom when the military arrived. Aside from the thousands of servicemen who moved to Churchill, there was an influx of civilian personnel. Some worked at the base and others started new businesses to meet the needs of this population explosion. The town also depended on the base for light, power, fire fighting equipment, road construction, medical facilities, and schools.

By 1964 both American and Canadian troops had pulled out and left the base to the Federal Department of Public Works. Scientific work, maneuvers, and survival training were still carried on there until the last serviceman left in 1980.

Manitoba Archives

This complex of buildings was once a military base that housed close to 4,500 servicemen and support staff. It was leveled by bulldozers in 1981 (p. 20). Churchill airport links Manitoba and the South to the Keewatin District of the Northwest Territories.

D. LeGros

The last rocket was fired in 1985 from the NRC's Churchill Rocket Range. An aerial view of the Rocket Range shows the many small lakes that are typical of Manitoba's geography.

22

By that time the town of Churchill's Redevelopment Program had built housing and a recreational and health centre, and activity had shifted away from the base. In 1981 the multimillion-dollar base was demolished, leaving only the airport, fire station, hydro plant, and a few other buildings as reminders of the glory that was once Fort Churchill.

The fire and light of the aurora borealis fills the sky over Churchill with astonishing frequency. Their erratic dance is accompanied by changing colors in fall and winter. The aurora is about 125 kilometres (80 miles) above the ground but local lore has it that if you whistle at the aurora it will make them dance and come down to the ground. This is the place to see them. Churchill is located in the zone where the greatest incidence of northern lights occurs. That and its remoteness from civilian populations made it a perfect choice for a rocket range designed to explore the mysteries of the aurora and other astronomical phenomena.

Churchill had served the cause of astronomy before, in 1768, when an astral observatory was established at the as-yet-uncompleted Fort Prince of Wales, to study the transit of Venus across the Sun.

The first rocket launched to mark the international geophysical year in 1957 brought such excellent results that the U.S. Air Force built a permanent range. Jointly funded by NASA and Canada's National Research Council, the rocket range was an integral part of the town for 25 years, launching over 3,400 weather and research rockets, until the final countdown on May 8, 1985. Many of the townspeople turned out to observe the launch that marked the end of yet another era with an appropriate puff of smoke.

Ice on the placid Churchill River.
Northern lights in the Churchill sky (p. 23).

D. LeGros

Who goes there?

In 1982, Churchill went Hollywood — or vice versa. A movie company braved the elements in mid-winter in order to film the science fiction film "Iceman." Director Fred Schepski and crew chose the old rocket range for their set and augmented their Hollywood cast of Timothy Hutton, Lindsay Krauss, and James Tolkan with a number of local people. Despite the constant winds that howl around Churchill in winter, the crew had to use giant wind machines to whip up the snow in the approved Hollywood fashion.

D. LeGros

The Iceman *movie set.*
The sun attempts to break through the fury of a midwinter white-out.

Another visitor of note was the good ship, *Aquastar*, which became, in 1985, the first sailing ship to dock in Churchill in nearly 80 years. The ship, captained by Leslie Sike and crewed by his wife Carolann, along with Gay Curry and David Farr, made the journey from Toronto in 108 days. Their voyage was not all smooth sailing. Five bad storms hit them, the worst in the middle of Hudson Bay, where winds were clocked up to 60 knots and waves reached 6 metres (20 feet) high. For five days the *Aquastar* drifted helplessly in the relentless storm, sails and engine both useless. It was also stuck in the ice for three days off the Labrador coast and twice more in Ungava Bay. Not unreasonably, they demurred making the return trip under sail, preferring to send the ship back to Toronto on board a tugboat. Their historic voyage earned them the International Sailing World's Offshore Medal for excellence in sailing.

The Churchill Harbor is subjected to the largest tides in Hudson Bay, reaching 5 metres (16 feet) between high and low tide. As the powerful saltwater tide forces its way into the mouth of the Churchill River it propels the fresh water of the Churchill River back upstream. A distinct line becomes visible where the fresh and saltwater meet. You can straddle this line in a boat and taste the difference off each side of the boat (see photograph on p. 11).

*The **Aquastar** arrives at port.*

Everyone loves a mystery

Of the many thousands of visitors to Churchill, the one who caused the biggest stir was undoubtedly Lucky Lindy. It was in 1931, while the port was still under construction, that world famous pilot Charles Lindbergh and his wife Ann Morrow made a stopover in Churchill on their flight to the Orient. The roar of Lindbergh's plane as it came in for a landing was sufficient to empty the mess hall of most of the 2000 plus workers. They crowded the unfinished dock, hoping for a glimpse of the man who made the first nonstop trans-Atlantic flight.

The following year brought another visitor. Angus MacIver, then a 2-year resident of Churchill and sometime guide for tourists, took the stranger across the river to Fort Prince of Wales. MacIver found the man's behavior suspicious. He refused to give his name, saying it wasn't a good idea in his line of business, but claimed to be a reporter for the *Chicago Herald*. He also denied his accent was German, saying he was Norwegian. At the fort, the man was obsessively interested in the north wall, taking many photos from both the inside and outside. He was out of MacIver's sight for up to an hour and refused to say what he had been doing, despite MacIver's anger at being kept waiting until the tides were at a dangerous level. His final, enigmatic comment before departing was, "I make good money with canoe."

Two years later, MacIver saw a picture on the front page of the newspaper which he said looked like his mysterious stranger. The picture was of Bruno Hauptmann, the man who was convicted of kidnapping the Lindbergh baby. Some $20,000 of the ransom (in U.S. gold certificates) was not recovered. MacIver believes that Hauptmann may have buried it near the north wall of the fort and sent his photos to an accomplice who would then have recovered the loot.

Is this a likely tale? Hauptmann was known to have been in Canada between the kidnapping and his arrest, but no record of his visiting Manitoba was uncovered by the investigators. On the other hand, there are some who believe Hauptmann was merely a hapless accessory who took the fall for the real kidnappers. One of the witnesses who had dealt with one of the kidnappers, said he wasn't sure if Hauptmann was the man he met, but that he looked like him. He also recalled that the kidnapper denied his accent was German, claiming to be Norwegian. (Hauptmann's own English was so bad it could not really be construed as a mere accent.) It is also thought that the kidnappers made good their escape by canoe.

Would-be treasure hunters should be warned that the gold certificates would be worthless today and that Fort Prince of Wales is a National Park and the Superintendent of Parks would not take kindly to someone digging up the grounds.

Lindbergh and his wife at Churchill.

H. Wilson

How can you live where there aren't any trees?

Close-up of red bearberry plants. The labrador tea plant is the green in the background.

Crimson carpet of deciduous growth in autumn.

A lot of people will tell you that the subarctic is a barren wasteland, a cold expanse of icy white in winter, and a bleak, unbroken line of gray the rest of the year.

Of course, those people have never been here.

During the short, intense summer, a bewildering variety of wild flowering plants spring from the tundra soil in a veritable kaleidoscope of colors and delicate shapes. Come fall, the ground is a scarlet carpet of bearberries, interspersed with the downy white tufts of the arctic avens.

Peeking out from amid the riot of color is the green of the labrador tea plant, known in Cree as *wishekapacwaw*, which means "making of bitter liquid." Despite this rather derogatory name, the tea made from the leaves and flowers of the plant is not only pleasant tasting, but rumored to provide relief from rheumatism, stomach ache, and headache.

D. LeGros

Indian paintbrush.

Bright red soapberry.

D. LeGros

Arctic avens.

Labrador tea in full summer bloom.

The arctic aven changes from spring's bright yellow to feathery white in autumn (top right).

The arctic willow on an isolated shoreline rock (below right).

B. Turner

D. LeGros

The wild arctic sweet pea or **Hedysarum mackenzii** *develops pink and red blossoms throughout summer.*

32   Even the fierce winter itself creates Christmas-card-perfect landscapes. And that's despite the forceful winds off the bay making the few trees rather one-sided, so that in Churchill it takes two trees to make a Christmas tree.

Some ominous reminders of the forces of nature have become unlikely tourist attractions around Churchill. A C-46 freight plane, nicknamed "Miss Piggy" for its ability to carry an over-abundance of freight, still lies where it crashed in 1979, 1 kilometre (2/3 mile) north of Churchill Airport. No sooner had the plane left Churchill than it called in a "May Day" and tried to return. It was approaching the runway when it crashed. It's a testament to the skill of its pilot that no one on board was injured in the crash.

Another subject of many a vacation snapshot is the wreck of the *MV Ithaca,* which lies just off Bird Cove, 17 kilometres (11 miles) east of Churchill. In 1961 it was unceremoniously deposited on the tidal flats by the fickle winds and tides of Hudson Bay. Though stripped of all useful fittings and rusting badly, it nonetheless allows Churchill to boast a resident cargo freighter that stays year round.

Sparse coniferous forest of the taiga.
Wreck of "Miss Piggy."
Wreck of the **Ithaca** *(p. 33).*

The bay itself gets into the act of making marvelous things that appeal to the eye. At spring breakup, low tide deposits ice floes that have been eroded by river current and tides into fantastic ice sculptures.

The tide also cuts new, often intriguing designs into the shoreline every 11.5 hours. There are also eye-arresting geological phenomena. Rock on the shores of the bay, dated at 2 billion-years old, has been pummelled into smooth, flowing patterns by the incessant pounding of the waves.

Ice on Hudson Bay (p. 35). D. LeGros
The grain elevator is dwarfed by the tide-stranded ice floe.

*As the river ice breaks up hundreds of birds arrive.
Here eider ducks glide amongst ice floes bound for
Hudson Bay (p. 36).*

B. Turner

Rock sculptures made by wind and saltwater.

Mosaics in the sand crested by tidal run-off.

Bird watchers go into throes of ecstasy in Churchill. Close to 150 species of birds congregate there each summer and fall, including the tundra swan, horned grebe, snowy and short-eared owls, golden plover, arctic loon, snow goose, and the ubiquitous sandpiper.

And perhaps dearest to the birder's heart, is the Ross's gull. This little bird made the cover of *Time* magazine when it first successfully nested in North America. Rarely seen straying beyond its traditional nesting ground in Siberia, it was a thrill to nature lovers everywhere when it chose Churchill as its new home.

One of the most abundant species in the area, the willow ptarmigan stays year round in Churchill, its perfect summer camouflage of brown plumage changing to a snowy white in winter.

Perhaps the most fascinating summer visitor is the arctic tern which makes an incredible 21,000-kilometre (13,000-mile) migration from pole to pole twice a year, thus receiving more hours of sunlight than any other creature on earth.

The rare horned grebe nests in the Churchill area.

Manitoba Dept. of Natural Resources (MDNR)

The willow ptarmigan blends with autumn rusts and browns.
Ptarmigan gather on the snow of the tundra.
Ptarmigan in flight over the taiga.

D. LeGros

The semi-palmated sandpiper (p. 40).

Ross's gulls nest in Churchill. The tiny chicks become graceful birds with rosy breast, distinctive black neckband, and wedge-shaped tail.

MDNR

MDNR

MDNR

M. Macri

The arctic loon's deep red eye is part of his mating colors.
Mating arctic terns.

D. LeGros

An immature snow goose on the variegated tundra.

The golden plover nests on the arctic tundra. Here it performs the broken wing routine to lure predators away from its nest.

L. Skibo

Tundra swans.

Snowy owl with freighter in distance.
An immature short-eared owl.

MDNR

D. LeGros

MDNR

Though the animals that call the tundra home are rightfully wary of humans, they can often be glimpsed in the wild. Red, white, and silver fox are seen near town just after the first snowfall. Dark furred weasels change to lustrous white ermine come winter time. Ringed seals appear in the Churchill River in spring, and even the mighty caribou occasionally venture as far south as Churchill on their annual migratory route.

Tundra or barrenground caribou prefer the open ground, which distinguishes them from their southern cousins, the woodland caribou. One of the herds, the Kaminuriak, which makes up the tundra caribou, has dwindled from 150,000 to about 35,000 due to over-hunting by man in the 60s and 70s. Thanks to conservation practices and reduced animal kills, the herd now numbers around 250,000. It's been 30 years since caribou ranged near Churchill. One reason is that the moss they love to graze on takes nearly 30 years to grow back after the herds have ranged there.

The ringed seal arrives in the spring and suns itself on the ice.

48

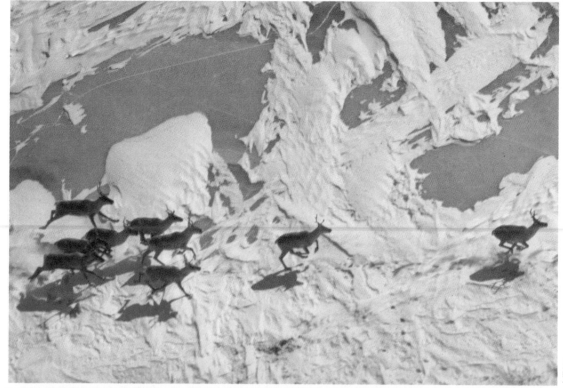

MDNR

Caribou sometimes venture as far south as Churchill.

Photographs on pages 46 and 47
courtesy of Manitoba Department of
Natural Resources (MDNR)

*A lone caribou is silhouetted against the tundra in the
Cape Churchill area.*

As many as 5,000 beluga whales populate Hudson Bay with up to 3,000 frequenting the Churchill River in order to feed on the small fish that teem there and to calve in the warmer water. The belugas, like much of the wildlife in the area, played a reluctant role in the development of Churchill. As early as the 1700s the Hudson's Bay Company recognized the importance of the area as a source of whale product. Whaling continued until the 1960s, with as many as 450 animals caught each year. As the demand for whale products decreased and public outcry at whaling increased, the number of kills per year has dropped dramatically, with only the occasional hunter receiving special permission to take a whale.

P. Watts

Beluga whales at the mouth of the Churchill River.

Only one organization, Nanuk Enterprises of Churchill, headed by John Hickes, has official authority to capture live whales for marine life zoos such as Marineland and Sea World. Original attempts at capturing the whales with power boats and nets proved unsuccessful. It wasn't until Hickes and his partner Francis Spence literally jumped onto a whale's back and stopped it by hanging onto its head and tail, that they were able to secure it with a rope. This catch-as-catch-can method is still in operation today and Hickes and his team are known as "white water cowboys."

Once secured, the whales are fitted into a sheep's wool-lined canvas stretcher and hauled back to a large holding tank filled with constantly circulating saltwater from the river estuary. Specially fitted chartered aircraft are used for transporting the belugas to their new homes at sites around the world, where it is reported, they adapt quickly to their new environments. Their natural curiosity and sociability remains undimmed and they apparently enjoy contact with their human trainers and keepers.

K. Hanley, *Hartford Courant*

L. Skibo

Isn't that where the polar bears live?

Churchill's fame as the Polar Bear Capital of the World is due to the town's proximity to the bears' traditional winter migration route and because the taiga region just south of the town is one of the largest polar bear denning areas on earth. As many as 100 pregnant females make their way there to spend the winter, emerging in the spring with between 150 and 200 cubs.

Another 500 to 600 bears gather every autumn in the Cape Churchill area on the shores of Hudson Bay, between the Churchill and Nelson Rivers, just 64 kilometres (40 miles) east of the town of Churchill. There they wait for the bay to freeze so they can cross the ice to hunt the ringed, ranger, or harbor seals that live there.

As summer food sources are scarce for the bears, they are driven by a hunger that often leads them into the town of Churchill itself, looking for the easy pickings afforded by the town dump just 10 kilometres (6 miles) from the outskirts of town. In fact this local garbage dump is where tourists still go to see bears, so it's likely the most visited dump in the world.

Some bold or inexperienced bears sometimes wander farther into town. This has made man-bear encounters all too common, with occasionally comic, but too often tragic results. In response to these encounters a polar bear control program was instituted in the late 1960s by Natural Resources Wildlife Management personnel, and the "Bear Patrol" is a common sight in the streets of Churchill.

The annual bear invasion has sparked a tourist boom, visitors coming from all over the world to participate in polar bear safaris. Journalists, photographers, wildlife specialists, and tourists with an enthusiasm for the adventurous board tundra buggies — specially constructed vehicles designed to ride high over the muskeg and, theoretically, out of reach of the bears. Armed with cameras they are chauffered to the areas that bears are known to frequent for a first-hand glimpse of these monarchs of the North.

D. LeGros

It's not only the tourists who are fascinated with these great white bears. When the new Churchill Tourist Information Centre was built, it seemed only natural to offset it with a lifesize sculpture of Churchill's most frequent visitor. A competition for best design was held, with entries being voted on by the local citizenry. They awarded the contract to renowned Winnipeg architect and scultor, Leo Mol, whose weathered bronze rendering of a mother and cub captures the paradoxical nature of the bear — graceful and playful, yet with a ferocious strength and durability.

A female with cubs and a male polar bear share the same whale meal (p. 55). M. Macri

Photograph on page 54 courtesy of
Dr. Lorraine Skibo.

Polar bear and cub sculpture by Leo Mol.

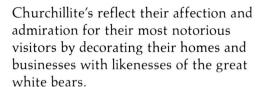

Churchillite's reflect their affection and admiration for their most notorious visitors by decorating their homes and businesses with likenesses of the great white bears.

The most important polar bear sign shows up every September when the Wildlife Natural Resources Management officers install the bright orange Polar Bear Alert signs to designate areas where bear encounters are likely to occur.

The leading lady of polar beardom is undoubtedly Linda, a.k.a. Bear Number 33, X 505. Her first visit to Churchill was as a 3-year old in 1966 when she attempted to enter a house. She was discouraged from her house-breaking by a tranquilizer dart and then airlifted out. Undeterred, she returned yearly, often with a cub or two in tow. She's been captured 21 times and sentenced to polar bear jail 4 times since the facility opened in 1980. Most of her dozen or so cubs have turned into problem bears and had to be either deported to zoos or destroyed.

Linda's own luck was up after her fourth incarceration in 1985. Or maybe not. She and her two cubs wound up basking (and eating regularly) in the zoo at Albuquerque, New Mexico.

Nancy Mutaten was at home with her four children and one grandchild on a cold October night in 1981 when a polar bear tried to break down her back door. She grabbed a shotgun and fired right through the door. The bear was forever cured of its habit of dropping in unexpectedly.

A member of an airline ground crew was guiding a plane into the airport and becoming increasingly confused by the pilot who not only refused to follow his directions but kept flashing his lights at him. Exasperated, the crewman looked around and found that he had company in the form of a full-grown bear, standing on its hind legs, less than 2 metres (6 feet) away. The man made a beeline for the underbelly of the plane, the pilot loudly revved his engines, and the bear suddenly recalled he had business elsewhere.

Husky Harris was once asked about the bloodstains on his toque. He tells of how he was sleeping on his boat anchored 60 metres (200 feet) out in the water and was awakened by something brushing against his face. He opened his eyes to find a bear looming over him. He'd known there were bears in the area which is why he'd chosen to sleep away from shore, with a gun by his side. On seeing the bear he reached for his gun, which, it turned out, was still in its cover. Husky couldn't ever explain why he spent precious time taking the cover off the gun before firing, but he did.

He did it quick though, and fired point-blank. He had just enough time to roll out of the way before the dead bear crashed onto the deck, sparing him from "having to spend the rest of the night under a ton of bear." That's how the bear's blood stained his toque and it was still there 5 years later. I wonder if Husky washed his socks more often than he washed his toque!

Not all polar bear stories end so happily for the humans involved. One such incident occurred some 20 years ago, before the region south of Churchill was known to be a polar bear denning area. A group of trappers were working in the area and one of them, John Spence, was checking the traplines when he came across a mother bear and two cubs. The bear immediately attacked and tore his arm severely. It took a day and a half to get the injured man back to Churchill. The arm was in such bad shape that it had to be amputated when he got to the hospital.

Then there's the story of a regular visitor to Churchill, Fred Treul, a businessman from Milwaukee, Wisconsin, with a passion for photographing the bears. He was doing just that, leaning out of the door of a tundra buggy (some 4 metres or 12 feet from the ground), when a bear crept up unnoticed from below and behind him and fastened its teeth in his arm. The bear did some damage, but Treul has recovered full use of his arm. He was back in Churchill the following year, boarding the tundra buggy with camera in hand and saying how good it was to be getting back on the tundra again.

At age 37, Sonny Voisey was a seasoned hunter, trapper, and fisherman who had every reason to believe he was skilled in the ways of surviving in the northern wilderness. However a fishing trip with five of his buddies nearly brought Sonny's life to a premature end.

He had left his friends fishing near their camp and gone off with a .22 rifle in search of geese. "I came across a set of big fresh bear tracks, and I mean big bastards," he recounts, "but I didn't see any bear. I heard two rifle shots from the direction of the tents so I figured maybe they'd scared the bastard away."

He started back, staying close to the water, knowing a bear might be hiding in the bushes. But the way to the camp took him close by some bushes and he unknowingly walked right by a 400-kilogram (900-pound) bear. He turned when it snorted and got to its feet. Then it charged him.

Sonny ran, shouting for his friends and heading for the water, hoping to get into an open area so the others could get a shot at it. He knew that a shot from his .22 wouldn't do much more than make the bear madder, so he threw the rifle behind him, hoping the bear might stop to smell it. No such luck.

The bear kept coming and Sonny, knowing he had no hope of outrunning it, fell on his stomach and tried unsuccessfully to protect his head.

"The bear seemed to fit my whole head in his mouth and I thought, 'you gotta go sometime, but what a way to go.' It bit right close to my right ear so it felt and sounded like my whole skull was being crushed. Then it lifted me and shook me like a rag doll. I guess when it grabbed me I tightened my neck muscles for all they were worth because it didn't break my neck."

His friends were watching but couldn't shoot for fear of hitting Sonny. So, Sonny played dead. The bear believed him. It rolled him around with its paws, then seized his head again and began dragging him back toward its bed. Then it stopped and put one huge paw on his back.

"I thought to myself, this is it now. I love you God and I love you Mom." Then the bear started to drag him again.

Sonny's friends also believed he was dead and opened fire. The bear continued dragging his captive after being hit once. A second hit convinced it to let go. It took two more shots to kill it.

Sonny never lost consciousness during the 45-minute trek back to Churchill. From there he was evacuated by air ambulance to Winnipeg for extensive surgery and a 3-month hospital stay.

He attributes his survival to the fact that he didn't panic and played dead. He still hunts and fishes in the wilds outside Churchill and his enthusiasm for the way of life he loves remains undampened.

There are two legacies from his experience. One is that he's "a little bit more careful now. It won't happen to me again, that's for sure." The other is the scars on his head, about which he says, "I hope I don't go bald later, 'cause if I do, I'm going to need a wig to hide those scars."

Sonny Voisey and polar bear.

What do you do up there, anyway?

Life in Churchill, as anywhere else, is what you make it — once you've taken into account both the limitations and the opportunities offered by the weather and the surrounding wilderness. The character of the community is dictated not just by these ungovernable forces, but by the diverse nature of its citizens, some of whom are living on their ancestral turf while others of widely diverging backgrounds have chosen Churchill as their home.

Some of Churchill's population live much as their ancestors did — by hunting, fishing, and trapping. For the most part, though, they've long since traded in their igloos and dogsleds for sturdy wooden houses (albeit sometimes without running water) and fast, powerful snowmobiles — often to the disappointment of romantic Southern visitors who hoped to see the pictures in the history books come to life.

While the old ways are important to the Inuit, the people now embrace the best of modern technology. The Churchill Health Centre's hospital is equipped with short- and long-term care facilities, obstetric, emergency, dental, and social services. Because the hospital services the Keewatin District of the Northwest Territories which includes close to 6000 people, the Churchill hospital has a patient list that is 50 to 75 percent Inuit.

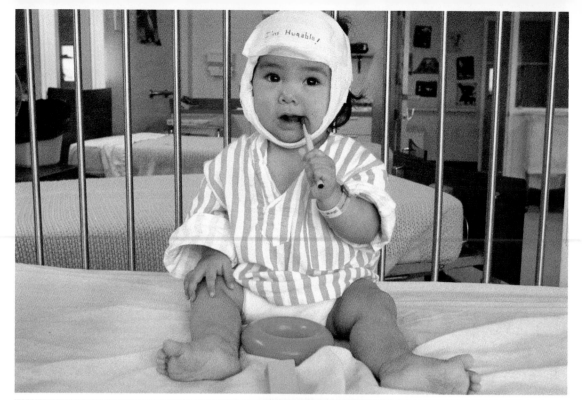

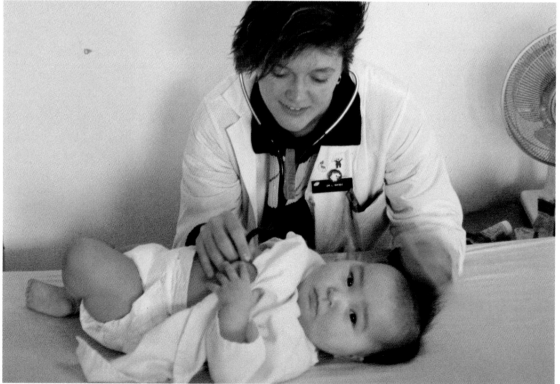

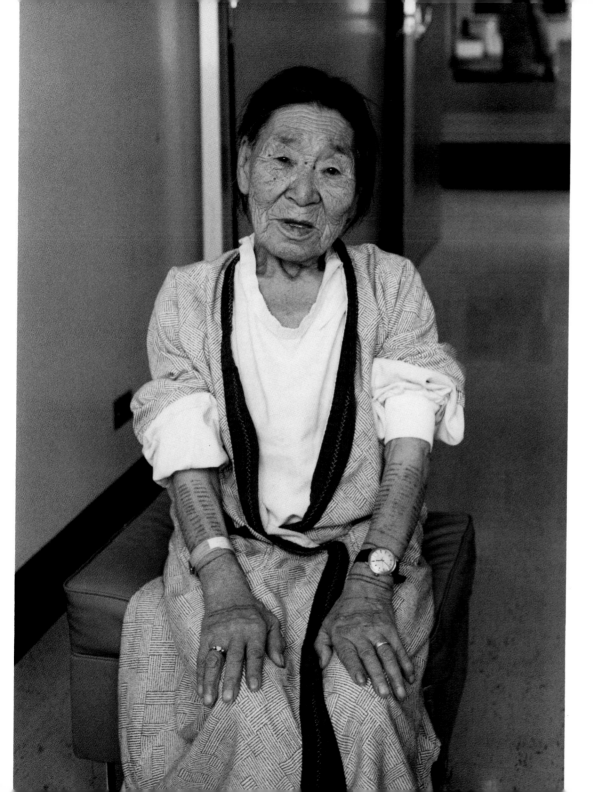

Rosalie Nanorak, an 85 year-old Inuk (singular for Inuit) is one of the few women left in the North whose face, hands, legs, and arms are adorned with tatoos. This was a time-honored custom, usually begun a year or so before marriage and completed a year or so afterwards. The tatoo patterns are intricate and must have been painful to do, but women submitted to them willingly. Today's Inuit women, however, prefer make-up, earrings, and necklaces and no longer are tatooed.

Mina Aqiatusuk is also an Inuit affected by the white man's culture. This little girl was born in a modern hospital in Churchill and her place of birth is listed as Manitoba even though she will spend the rest of her life in the Northwest Territories. It's the modern practice to bring the mothers out of their communities for the delivery. The women miss their families and the eventual goal of the Community Health Councils of the Inuit communities served by Churchill is to have midwives available in each settlement in the North.

Traditional craftsmanship survives, however. Myrtle DeMeulles is the proprietor of the Arctic Sewing Centre where she and her staff turn animal skins and pelts into beautifully beaded clothing. Their work is sold as far away as Banff, Alberta, and even Italy. Their specialty is filling custom orders including, on one occasion, a $3,000 white fox bedspread.

"There is a millionaire from down south who comes up every year and asks me to make him something out of skunk fur," says a bemused Myrtle. "I've made him a parka, mitts, and a hat, so I can't help but wonder what he'll want next."

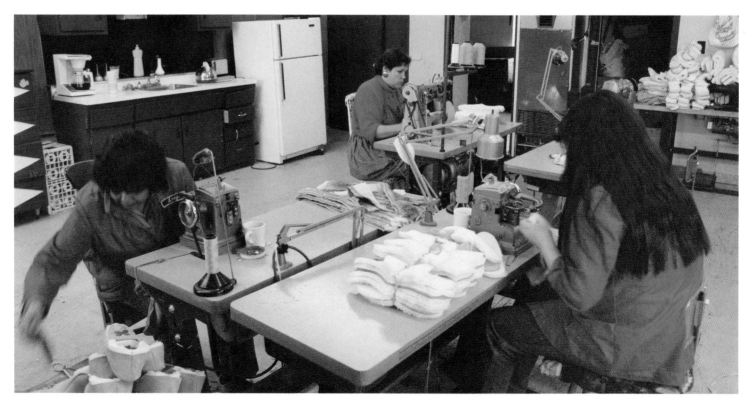

Keith Rawlings.

Non-native newcomers have often championed northern culture. The late Keith Rawlings was instrumental in starting the sewing centre with DeMeulles and was also the force behind the Arctic Trading Post. A British immigrant, Rawlings came to the North as a cook for a construction crew in the Northwest Territories in the 1950s. He fell in love with the North and, with his wife Penny, built the trading post in 1978. With its pot-bellied stove and walls decorated with animal skins, the store evokes memories of its frontier counterparts. The hand-made products of the Arctic Sewing Centre share shelf space with souvenir doodads, soapstone carvings, handi-crafts, and work by artists from all areas of northern Canada.

The Rawlings' also opened the Trader's Table restaurant, which offers tourists and locals alike a taste of real Northern cooking.

Keith Rawlings met an untimely end when a plane he was traveling in crashed at Rankin Inlet, Northwest Territories, in November, 1986.

68   The crash that killed Keith Rawlings claimed the life of Bishop Robidoux whose Churchill home base was the jumping off point for his 3.8 million square kilometre (1.5 million square mile) diocese. In his 16-year residence in Churchill, Bishop Robidoux was deeply involved with the Inuit. Later he became a sort of spokesman for the fur traders who were facing a huge anti-fur movement. He was also instrumental in forging the plans for the Churchill Town Complex, opposing those who wanted to cut back on some of the amenities, insisting it was important for not just the present generation but future generations of Churchill. A plaque honoring Bishop Omer Robidoux was erected in November, 1987, in the town complex.

The late Jacques-Marie Volant was another member of the clergy who worked toward the preservation of Inuit culture. The Eskimo Museum was his labor of love from the time when he assisted in its construction in 1948. The museum presents not only an exquisite collection of contemporary Inuit art but also sections devoted to the history of the Inuit and life in the Arctic.

Churchill's Roman Catholic church, the Holy Canadian Martyrs Church, was one of the first buildings constructed in Churchill that was not related to the Churchill port. The Oblate Order established a mission in 1929 and in 1931 work began on the church and rectory. The completed church became the Bishop's cathedral for the Hudson Bay diocese. The church continues its work today under the direction of Father Dufour.

At the front of the cathedral is an intricate painted mural depicting the interaction between Christianity and the Inuit and Indian people. It was painted by the original Oblate priests in the area.

Sigrun Martin remembers the early days of the mission. "We loved Christmas at the mission back then. Everyone would get together for a Christmas feast. It is one of my fondest memories of my childhood in Churchill."

The story of St. Paul's Anglican Church reveals another chapter in Churchill's unique history. In 1882 the Reverend J. J. Lofthouse was dispatched from England to set up a mission at Churchill. He spent a couple of years at York Factory so it was 1885 before he began conducting church services at Churchill. His church was both residence for him and place of worship for his Indian and Hudson's Bay Company workers congregation. The church was so small that each Sunday he had to pack up his belongings to make room for the benches that were brought in to seat the congregation.

In 1889 an 8 x 16 metre (25 x 50 ft) prefabricated church was ordered from England. It arrived in 1890 but it took 3 years to put it all together. It is still in use today.

A sunny afternoon invites locals out for a chinwagging session in Hudson Square.

Children in Churchill are the same as children everywhere — they can't keep their shoes on or their pants done up.

Most of Churchill has modern housing today, but some native families prefer the independence of owning their own homes. This house along the river flats has electricity but no running water.

Although igloos are a rare occurrence in the Churchill region today they are occasionally built by winter hunters and trappers.

Living in the North requires ingenuity. A covered sled protects the children from the bitter winds and cold temperatures.

Churchill is a spot of dry land in a vast expanse of ocean and bog. The town itself is built on the solid rock foundation of the Hudson Bay coastline but the soil shifts constantly as a result of permafrost. Traditional telephone poles don't work but these curious tripods provide Churchill's link with the South.

Dog sledding is not entirely a thing of the past. Brian Ladoon has seen to that. Ladoon, one of northern Canada's foremost painters, is also one of the few breeders of championship pure-bred Canadian Eskimo dogs.

Ladoon has lived most of his life in Churchill, except for a few years spent as a merchant seaman, visiting ports of call in Europe, Africa, and South America. A hunter, trapper, and fisherman as well, Ladoon seems like a character out of an adventure novel. More than that, he exemplifies those who chose Churchill as home before the town's industrial revolution in the 1930s. Though mainly occupied with his dogs and his art, Ladoon still makes some of his living from the land as a hunter, crossing the tundra and taiga by dogsled.

Brian Ladoon in his studio and with his championship dogs.

D. LeGros

Boris Oszurkiewicz arrived in Churchill from his native Poland in the 1950s and decided he was home. Perhaps his passion for the wide open spaces of the Far North was, in part, a reaction to the time he spent in a German concentration camp during World War II. Boris is a trapper, a profession that some people consider is only for the hard-hearted. They might have changed their mind had they seen Boris and his fox pup. The under-aged fox who got his foot caught in one of Boris' traps was too young for his pelt to be of any value. Boris would have released him, but the little fellow's foot was injured. In an ironic twist, the hunter wound up nursing his little captive back to health.

Sigrun Martin (nee Sigurdson) has the distinction of being one of the first women to live in Churchill. "When I came up in 1933 with my father, my mother, and 2 sisters, we more than doubled the female population of Churchill," she recalls. Until that time, no women were allowed in the area, in fear that the presence of females among the more than 2000 men working on constructing the port would prove a source of trouble.

The site of the Sigurdson's first house became the spot where the S & M supermarket now stands. The store's name comes from both the Sigurdson and Martin families who have enjoyed business as well as family ties since those early days when Sigrun and her sisters were the belles of Churchill.

Sigrun Sigurdson Martin.

Churchill's grain elevator towers over the compact townsite.

"Churchillites" tend to show a never-say-die attitude to most things. Take farming for instance. Despite a climate that is almost entirely inhospitable to agriculture, some locals are not only taking up the challenge, but succeeding to a good degree.

Bill and Diane Erickson operate the Boreal Gardens, experimenting with the cultivation of fruits, vegetables, and bedding plants. The long summer days are conducive to growing, but frost sets in by early September, so most of their plants are grown in greenhouses. These are heated by energy from the town grid which is fed by a huge, egg-beater-like wind-driven turbine erected by the National Research Council and currently under the auspices of the Department of Energy, Mines and Resources Canada and the Churchill Northern Studies Centre. In addition to offering the residents of Churchill fresh produce and working to find some of the answers to growing green things so close to the Arctic Circle, the Ericksons monitor the grid on a daily basis.

D. Erickson

D. Erickson

Malcolm Armstrong and the irrepressible Boris Oszurkiewicz are the poultry kings of Churchill. Malcolm is now bowing out, leaving the raising of about 100 chickens each summer to Boris. The cold winter winds make the chickens' skin feel and taste like rubber, so few of the fat white fowls strutting in the yard ever see the first days of autumn.

Malcolm and Boris join a long line of those who have tried to raise livestock in Churchill. They are having more success than the would-be cattlemen and horse ranchers — and certainly better luck than Johnny Bilenduke had with his attempt to raise hogs.

"I remember chasing bears away a half-a-dozen times one day," says Bilenduke after discovering that the polar bear population considered his pen full of hogs to be a pork chop buffet provided just for them. "One day the bears learned to climb my chain link fence and that was the end of my hog-farming days."

Malcolm Armstrong's chickens don't like the cold nights of Churchill's summer. Their joints get so stiff the chickens stagger in the morning as if they're drunk.

Many of Churchill's residents are employed by the Port of Churchill, including tugboat operators, grain handlers, dockworkers, and port maintenance men. One thing that the latter group have to deal with is ships that have sustained damage on the treacherous journey through the Hudson Strait and the Bay itself. The problem is one that the crew of the Titanic would recognize — submerged ice. The Titanic's nemesis was an iceberg, an ice mountain with at least one-tenth of its mass riding high above the water. It's the growlers, however, huge floes that lie mostly submerged, that do the most damage to ships, as Captain Christos Dezes of the freighter *Sea Link* will attest. Unfamiliar with Hudson Strait, and arriving early in the year, Dezes ran his ship afoul of a growler, which took a huge bite out of the *Sea Link's* bow. "The ice was deceptive. The piece we hit that did all the damage looked no larger than a small ice floe." The *Sea Link* received temporary repairs from the port maintenance crew before being loaded with grain and heading back to its home port.

At least ships are in safe hands once they arrive at the Port of Churchill. The *George Kidd* and the larger *H. M. Wilson* are the 2 tugboats that assist the ocean-going vessels in docking. A new tugboat with icebreaking capabilities has just been added to the fleet, replacing the *W. N. Twolan*, a tug captained by Wynford Goodman, that saw some 31 years service before being retired.

D. LeGros

80

As the spring days lengthen so too does the duration of the sunsets. By the summer solstice the longest day of the year in Churchill has about 20 hours of sunlight (p. 81).

The CN transports grain to the port.

A summer fog envelops the Port of Churchill during an early morning low tide.

82	It's not all work in Churchill. Residents know how to have fun and take advantage of their short summer. One important event is the celebration of Canada Day. This holiday is held every year across the country but Churchill's activities are perhaps the most unique. Denizens of other cities may make brief, brave forays into icy waters in mid-winter, but Churchill is, naturally, the true home of the Polar Bear Dip. (Real polar bears are not in attendance.)

At high tide each July 1, the beach is crowded with strangely garbed teams of people. Originality in costuming is *de rigeur* — and the rule is "the weirder the better." Then the games begin. This is no hasty dip. It is, in fact, a relay race, requiring each member of the team to plunge into 5°C (40°F) water and complete a trip to and from a preset marker — often situated near an accommodating ice floe. The winners are those who complete the course fastest. The losers — those who succumb to hypothermia. The presence of ice still in the bay deters neither the relay participants nor passionate windsurfers like Lorraine Skibo and Norbert Froese.

The tourism boom keeps many Churchill residents busy, and several have responded to the influx of visitors by creating innovative companies to serve them.

In 1979 local handyman Len Smith gathered together scrap metal and used car parts and created the first tundra buggy. From such inauspicious beginnings came a fleet of tundra vehicles used to carry tourists in search of polar bears. Operated by a variety of wildlife adventure companies, each buggy seats about 28 people and is equipped with heaters and on-board washrooms. The massive buggies move on 450-kilogram (nearly 1000-pound) tires which spread the immense weight of the vehicles.

From a height of nearly 5 metres (15 feet), they provide the best possible view of the bears in their natural habitat. Their fame has spread, and both *National Geographic* and *Life* magazines have featured the vehicles.

Another wildlife adventure that is popular with visitors is the whale safari conducted by Sea North tours. Mike and Doreen Macri started 12 years ago with one small boat. Now they operate full-time throughout the summer and early fall, using 2 boats with a combined capacity of 37 passengers.

Of particular interest are the huge pods of beluga whales, which yearly visit the mouth of the Churchill River by the thousands. The whales are sociable and curious, often breaching the water quite near the boats. Macri augments the visual experience with a hydrophone and amplifier which pick up and broadcast the whales' musical voices.

Aquatic birds seen nowhere else are in abundance, and ringed seals and polar bears can often be glimpsed in the area. In nice weather, Mike's been known to host a full-scale barbecue on a mid-river ice floe.

Mike Macri on an ice floe.

Halloween falls right in the middle of bear season. To protect the trick or treaters, Natural Resources personnel, RCMP, and volunteer fire fighters patrol the streets of Churchill constantly. Bears approaching the town are herded away with flare guns or tranquilized and captured. Bears actually entering the township will likely be shot to death. There is too much risk of the tranquilizer not working quickly enough to prevent an attack.

"X9640, X9171, X9247, and X3040 were all released from D-20 jail today on parole. X9640 was a first offender while the others had been arrested on previous occasions. At last report, all 4 were headed north. It is likely we will see one or 2 of them next year."

This is a crime report from the Churchill area. However, the criminals in question are polar bears and their crime was foraging for food too near civilization.

The D-20 jail was initiated in 1980 and is run by Natural Resources personnel, known locally as the Bear Patrol. The jail can hold up to 25 bears who are captured if they venture within the boundaries of the Polar Bear Control area.

MDNR

88   The bears are shot with tranquilizer guns, then transported via a culvert cage to polar bear jail where they stay until they can be released onto the ice-covered bay. Before their release they are weighed, measured, have a tooth pulled to determine their age, given an X number, and have another number dyed into the fur on their backs for easy identification from a distance.

The bears receive no food while in jail, since Natural Resource officers don't want the bears to get the idea that jail is a great place to be. When the animals wake up they are usually happy to leave the Churchill area at speed, heading north toward the ice and a good dinner.

Ian Thorleifson holds a drugged 80 kg (175 lb) bear in his arms.

This drugged bear is still aware of the presence of man.

MDNR

Not all bears are released near Churchill. In 1985, for example, there were 84 bears handled and the jail could only take 25. The others are airlifted by helicopters to the mouth of the Seal River, 64 kilometres (40 miles) north. The unconscious bears are placed in nets for their flights. They are blind-folded not because of a fear of heights but because the anaesthetic prevents their eyelids from working and sunlight could damage their eyes.

Churchill is much more than bears.
Yet it is the polar bear that
represents the spirit of the tiny
community. The strong independent
animal relies upon its instinct and
intelligence to survive in the North.
So too the people of Churchill have
pitted their wit and strength and
endurance against the elements to
prosper in this bleak and beautiful
land.

*Mist rises off the grainary ponds. These ponds are
loaded with nutrition from settling grain dust from
the elevator and provide food for hundreds of birds
that make their home during their summer stay.*

D. LeGros

Index